My New Pet

Guinea Pig

Jinny Johnson

A⁺

Smart Apple Media

Published by Smart Apple Media,
an imprint of Black Rabbit Books
P.O. Box 3263, Mankato, Minnesota, 56002
www.blackrabbitbooks.com

Printed in the United States of America,
at Corporate Graphics in North Mankato, Minnesota.

Designed by Guy Callaby
Edited by Mary-Jane Wilkins
Illustrations by Bill Donohoe

Library of Congress Cataloging-in-Publication Data

Johnson, Jinny, 1949-
Guinea pig / Jinny Johnson.
    p. cm. -- (My new pet)
Audience: K to grade 3.
Summary: "Describes life, features, and habits of guinea
pigs. Also helps children select a new pet"-- Provided by
publisher.
Includes index.
ISBN 978-1-62588-029-1 (library binding)
1. Guinea pigs as pets--Juvenile literature. I. Title.
SF459.G9J642 2014
636.935'92--dc23

                              2013002969

Photo acknowledgements
t = top, c = center, b = bottom
title page Denis Tabler/Shutterstock; page 2 Egor
Arkhipov/Shutterstock; 3t Dmitriy Shironosov,
b Kuttelvaserova/both Shutterstock; 7 iStockphoto/
Thinkstock; 8 Kristo-Gothard Hunor/Shutterstock;
10 Eric Isselée/Shutterstock; 11t magicoven, c Melisa
Mok Mun Chee, b cristi180884/all Shutterstock;
12 Vladimir L/Shutterstock; 13 Egor Arkhipov/
Shutterstock; 14 Jiri Hera/Shutterstock; 15t paintings,
b Imageman/both Shutterstock; 17 Hemera/Thinkstock;
18 Jinny Johnson; 23 TranceDrumer
Front cover: Hemera/Thinkstock

DAD0510
052013
9 8 7 6 5 4 3 2 1

Contents

I'm very excited. My mom says I can have a pet guinea pig.

I want to know all about guinea pigs so I can look after my pet well.

Here's what I have found out.

Guinea pigs

are small and plump, with short legs and sharp teeth.

They are **rodents**, like mice and hamsters.

Pet guinea pigs usually live for four or five years, but they can live as long as **eight years**.

Wild guinea pigs live in South America. They often shelter in burrows.

Guinea pigs like **company**.

We've decided to have two so they won't get lonely.

I will look for guinea pigs that have bright eyes and a clean nose and mouth. That shows they are **healthy**.

A guinea pig's coat should be smooth and glossy, too.

Before we get my guinea pigs, my dad and I will buy everything they need.

We will buy a big **cage** and special **bedding** to put inside it.

The cage will have a plastic base and a wire top.

We will also buy some **food bowls** and a **water bottle**.

I'm going to enjoy making my new pets' home ready.

They can hide and sleep under here.

First I will line the cage with **newspaper**.

Then I will put in some **wood shavings** to soak up the guinea pigs' pee.

On top of that I will put lots of **hay**. They will like snuggling up in that.

I know that it's very important to keep my pets **clean**.

Guinea pigs like to be gently **brushed and combed** to keep their coats clean.

Every day I will take any dirty or wet hay out of the cage. Then I'll put in some fresh hay.

Every week I will take everything out of the cage and **wash** the cage well.

I will buy some guinea pig **food** in the pet store. Every day I will give my pets food and **clean water**.

Guinea pigs like fresh food, too. I will give them treats such as celery, cucumber, and carrots.

Some foods aren't good for guinea pigs. I will check with mom and dad before giving my pets a new food.

I know I have to be **gentle** with my new pets at first.

I might give my pets a tasty snack like a strawberry to show I'm their friend.

Everything will be strange to them and they might be **frightened**.

I will let them get used to their new home before I try to touch them.

Guinea pigs need some **exercise** outside their cage.

In summer we will put a **pen** in the yard so they can run around on the grass safely.

In winter, I will let them out inside our house. I will watch them very carefully.

Hurray! I have my new guinea pigs.

They are both **female** and they are six weeks old.

I'm learning how to **hold** them very carefully with both hands so they feel safe.

My new pets are going to be very happy and so am I!

21

Notes for parents

Choosing a pet
Make sure you buy guinea pigs from a good pet store or breeder. Take the animals to the vet for a health check. Ask the vet to check the sex of the animals too. Pet stores sometimes get it wrong!

Handling and caring for guinea pigs
Show children how to pick up and hold guinea pigs very carefully. Teach them to respect animals and always treat them gently.

Health
It's up to you as a parent to make sure any pet is looked after properly. Supervise feeding and handling, especially at first. Keep an eye on the animal's health. Check its teeth and claws regularly and take the pet to the vet if they get too long.

Words to remember

burrow
A hole in the ground where an animal lives.

mammal
An animal that feeds its young with its own milk. Cats, dogs, guinea pigs, and people are all mammals.

rodents
A group of mammals that includes rats and mice, as well as guinea pigs, hamsters and gerbils.

mouse

Index